DATE DUE

CROSS-SECTIONS

THE AH–64 APACHE HELICOPTER

by Ole Steen Hansen
illustrated by Alex Pang
Consultant: Craig Hoyle, Defense Editor, Flight International

Capstone
press
Mankato, Minnesota

First published in the United States in 2006 by Capstone Press
151 Good Counsel Drive, P.O. Box 669, Mankato, Minnesota 56002
http://www.capstonepress.com

Library of Congress Cataloging-in-Publication Data
Hansen, Ole Steen.
   The AH-64 Apache helicopter / by Ole Steen Hansen ; illustrated by Alex Pang.
   p. cm.—(Edge books cross-sections)
   Summary: "An in-depth look at the AH-64 Apache helicopter, with detailed cross-
section diagrams, action photos, and fascinating facts"—Provided by publisher.
   Includes bibliographical references and index.
   ISBN 0-7368-5250-6 (hardcover)
   1. Apache (Attack helicopter)—Juvenile literature. 2. United States. Army—
Aviation—Juvenile literature. I. Pang, Alex, ill. II. Title.
UG1232.A88H36 2006
623.74'6047—dc22   2005009629

Designed and produced by

David West 🎎 Children's Books
7 Princeton Court
55 Felsham Road
Purney
London SW15 1AZ

Designer: Rob Shone
Editors: Gail Bushnell, Kate Newport

Photo Credits
Flight International, 4-5, 6-7, 10, 13, 16, 22b, 28-29; TRH Pictures, 22-23; Corbis,
20-21, 28; NASA, 29

1 2 3 4 5 6 10 09 08 07 06 05

TABLE OF CONTENTS

AH-64D LONGBOW APACHE

The Apache is the U.S. Army's attack helicopter. This deadly weapon can fight and destroy enemy tanks and other targets on the ground.

The Apache is fast. In just 30 minutes, it can fly 80 miles (130 kilometers) and destroy an enemy. Its top speed is 182 miles (300 kilometers) per hour.

The Apache performs well in the dark and even in bad weather. It is also designed to give its crew the best possible protection.

THE HELICOPTER GUNSHIP

The attack helicopter was made to protect other helicopters in combat.

BELL UH-1 IROQUOIS

The Vietnam War (1954–1975) was very much a helicopter war. The U.S. Army used helicopters to fly soldiers to combat areas. Helicopters were also used to take wounded soldiers to hospitals.

The Bell UH-1 Iroquois, or "Huey," was used for both of these jobs. The army soon decided that this helicopter needed protection against the enemy while it was working. It needed a combat helicopter to work as a flying bodyguard.

The UH-1 was often hit by enemy fire. More than 3,000 UH-1s were lost in Vietnam. These large losses led to the idea of an attack helicopter.

MIL MI-24 HIND

The Soviet Union saw how many U.S. helicopters were lost in Vietnam. They also decided to create a combat helicopter. They created the big and heavily armed Mil Mi-24 to carry soldiers and attack the enemy.

AH-1 HUEY COBRA

In the United States, the Bell company made the AH-1 Huey Cobra attack helicopter. It flew with transport helicopters to attack enemies. The U.S. Marine Corps will use new versions of the AH-1 until about 2020.

The Mi-24 carries rockets and missiles on small wings. The wings also help to lift the helicopter in forward flight just like the wings of an airplane.

The two-seat Huey Cobra helicopter was the world's first real attack helicopter. It proved how useful this kind of helicopter could be.

CROSS-SECTION

LONGBOW RADAR
See pages
18–19

COCKPIT
See pages
16–17

The AH-64A Apache first flew in 1975. Take a look inside the latest version, the AH-64D. The labels show which pages will help you to find out more.

The Apache has been constantly improved. The AH-64D model has the Longbow radar over the main rotor. The Longbow radar makes this modern helicopter even more dangerous.

AVIONICS
See pages 18–19

MACHINE GUN
See pages 24–25

AMMUNITION STORE
See pages 24–25

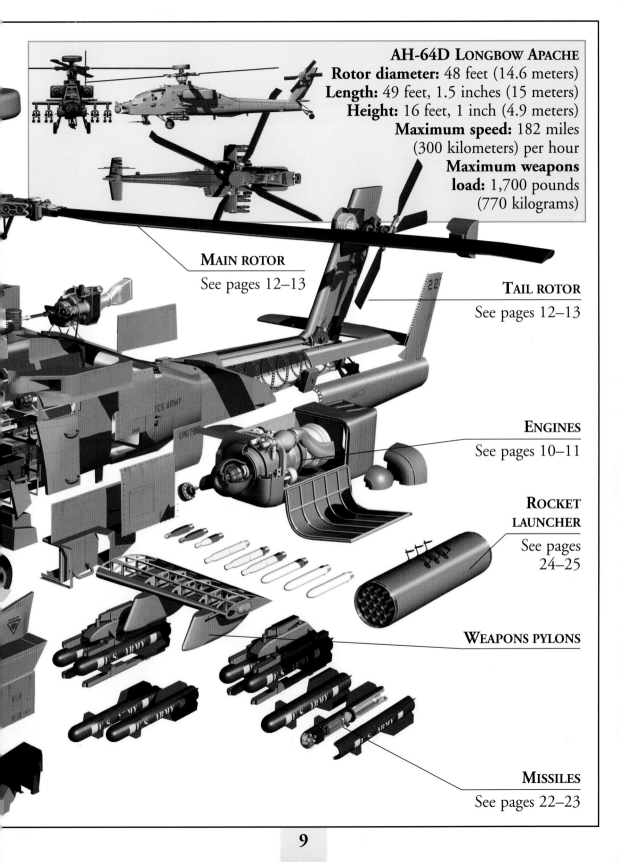

AH-64D Longbow Apache
Rotor diameter: 48 feet (14.6 meters)
Length: 49 feet, 1.5 inches (15 meters)
Height: 16 feet, 1 inch (4.9 meters)
Maximum speed: 182 miles
(300 kilometers) per hour
**Maximum weapons
load:** 1,700 pounds
(770 kilograms)

MAIN ROTOR
See pages 12–13

TAIL ROTOR
See pages 12–13

ENGINES
See pages 10–11

**ROCKET
LAUNCHER**
See pages
24–25

WEAPONS PYLONS

MISSILES
See pages 22–23

THE ENGINES

The Apache has two turboshaft engines. Having one on each side cuts down the risk of both engines being knocked out in one hit.

Armor plates protect the Apache's engines. But if one engine is knocked out, the Apache can fly back to base on only one engine.

The engines make the power to turn the rotors. The power is taken to the rotors through gears and transmission shafts. This system will work for one hour without oil if the Apache gets damaged in battle.

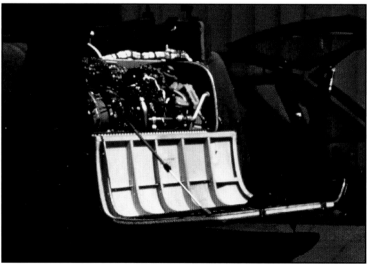

The engine covers fold down and become catwalks for the engineers.

AIR INTAKE
Engines work by sucking in air at the front, heating it up, and sending it out as hot exhaust. The exhaust turns a fan as it leaves the engine.

MAIN TRANSMISSION SHAFT
Strong shafts take the power from the engine to the gearbox.

AUXILIARY POWER UNIT
The Auxiliary Power Unit (APU) makes power on the ground when the big engines are not turning.

COMBUSTION CHAMBER
Fuel is burned in the combustion chamber in the center of the engine.

GEARBOX
A gear is needed between the shafts in the engines and rotors. This is because they turn at different speeds.

Position of engine on Apache

ENGINE SPECIFICATIONS
The AH-64D Longbow Apache has two General Electric T700-GE-701C turboshaft engines each rated at 1,800 horsepower (hp).

THE ROTORS

A plane's wings create lift, and its propellers pull it forward. On a helicopter, the main rotor has to do both jobs.

ROTOR HEAD

The rotor head can be moved in many different ways.

ROTOR BLADE

The rotor blades are very strong. They are made from titanium, stainless steel, and composites. They are built to keep working even when they are damaged.

The rotor blades are like rotating wings. Lift is created when air moves over them. The rotor also helps to control the helicopter. The Apache is more maneuverable than many other helicopters. Unlike most helicopters, the Apache can fly loops and rolls.

Position of rotors on Apache

TAIL ROTOR GEARBOX

The tail rotor gearbox controls the speed of the tail rotor.

TAIL ROTOR

The four rotor blades are set at an angle so that they make as little noise as possible.

TAIL ROTOR TRANSMISSION SHAFT

The tail rotor is turned by the transmission shaft, which is powered by the engines.

A four-bladed rotor is less noisy than a two-bladed rotor because it turns more slowly. The Apache's rotor is so quiet that enemies have a hard time hearing the helicopter coming.

The Apache's rotors have been designed to make as little noise as possible.

MANEUVERING

**A helicopter
can hover in the air.
It can also move forward,
backward, or sideways.**

Apache pilots use these moves to
hide behind hills, houses, rocks, or
trees so that they can surprise an
enemy. It is more difficult to control
a helicopter than an airplane.
Helicopters are especially hard to
control while they are hovering.

TORQUE
When the big rotor
turns, the helicopter
turns in the opposite
direction. The force that
makes this happen is
called torque. To avoid
this spinning, the
Apache has a tail rotor.
The tail rotor creates a
force in the opposite
direction to work
against the torque.

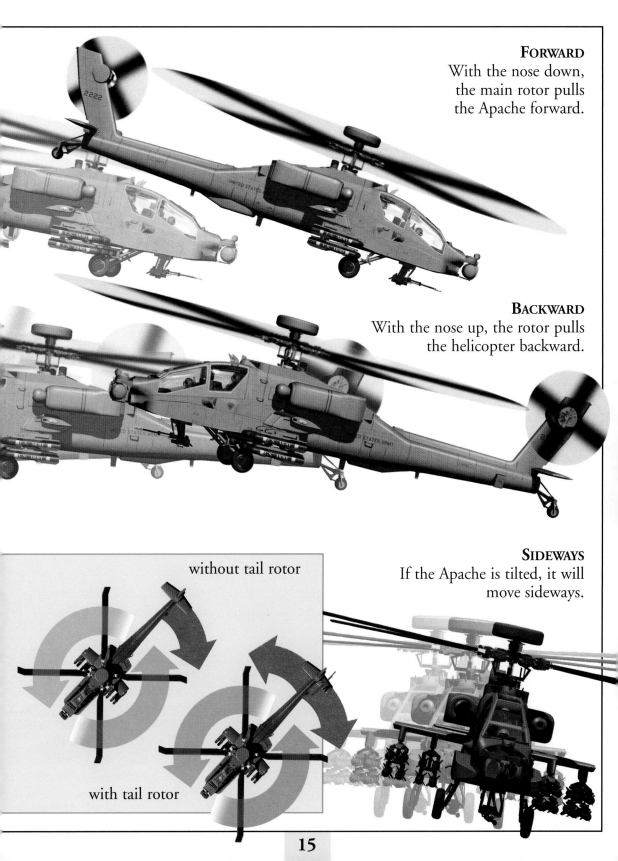

FORWARD
With the nose down, the main rotor pulls the Apache forward.

BACKWARD
With the nose up, the rotor pulls the helicopter backward.

SIDEWAYS
If the Apache is tilted, it will move sideways.

without tail rotor

with tail rotor

THE COCKPIT

The Apache has a two-person cockpit. The pilot sits behind the gunner.

The pilot sits higher than the gunner. The pilot needs a good view from the back seat.

The cockpit and its seats are armored. Armor protects the crew against handheld weapons and machine guns. In Vietnam, a large number of helicopters were shot down by these kinds of weapons.

The two cockpit areas are separated by an armored screen and a clear blast shield. The screen and shield reduce the risk of both crew members being killed or wounded at the same time.

The gunner fires the weapons. Should something happen to the pilot, the gunner can fly the helicopter. The pilot may also fire the weapons if the gunner is wounded.

Position of cockpit on Apache

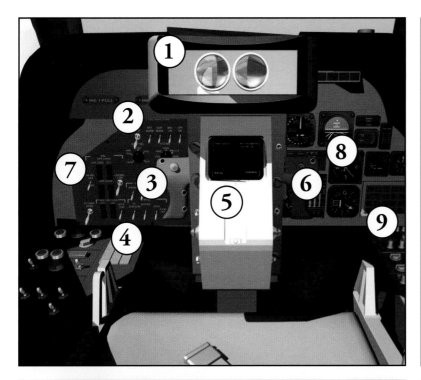

KEY TO GUNNER'S COCKPIT

1. Sensor eyepiece
2. Weapon arming switches
3. Weapon selection switch
4. Target selection switches
5. Video display
6. Laser tracking switches
7. Target control switches
8. Flight control dials
9. Warning lights panel

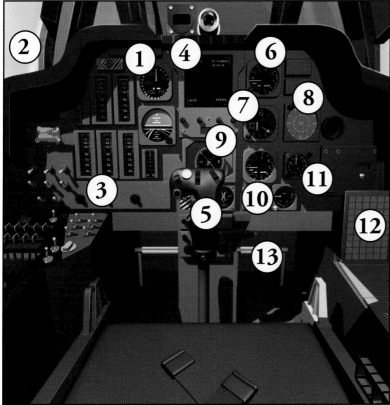

KEY TO PILOT'S COCKPIT

1. Airspeed indicator
2. Canopy
3. Fuel gauge and engine speed indicator
4. Video display
5. Control stick
6. Altimeter
7. Night flying altimeter
8. Radar display
9. Compass
10. Vertical speed indicator
11. Clock
12. Warning panel
13. Foot pedals

RADAR AND AVIONICS

All the electronics in an aircraft are called avionics. The Apache has advanced avionics to help the crew find its way, find the enemy, and aim its weapons.

The Longbow radar finds targets such as tanks, vehicles, radar sites, and missile launchers. The radar tracks up to 128 targets and finds out which are the most dangerous. It then suggests the top 16 targets.

Moving targets can be spotted up to 5 miles (8 kilometers) away. The Longbow radar can tell the difference between tracked and wheeled vehicles. It can find them hidden behind trees and brush.

PNVS

The Pilot Night Vision System (PNVS) lets the crew see, fly, and fight in the dark.

AVIONICS BAY

TADS

The Target Acquisition and Designation System (TADS) is used to find targets by day and night. The target can be shown on screens in the cockpit or on the IHADSS.

When the Apache is hidden, the radar only has to show for a second to find its targets.

Position of avionics on Apache

Signal to pilot's IHADSS

Signal to gunner's IHADSS

IHADSS

The Integrated Helmet And Display Sight System (IHADSS) is a small glass screen. It is fixed on the helmet in front of the eye. The screen gives important information, such as the location of targets, without the crew having to look at the instrument panels.

DEFENSE

The Apache has special defense equipment to make it difficult for enemy missiles to hit it.

Enemy aircraft might fire heat-seeking missiles that find the exhaust from the Apache. The exhaust is cooled to make it more difficult for missiles to find.

Enemies could also fire radar-controlled missiles at the Apache. Thin metal strips called chaff can be released by the Apache to confuse enemy radar. The Apache also uses a jammer that sends out signals to make the enemy radar think that the Apache is somewhere else.

CHAFF

Chaff are thin strips of metal foil that can be shot out.

FLARES

Flares may be fired to confuse heat-seeking missiles that will aim for the hot flares instead of the exhaust.

Apaches often work together with other aircraft. F-18s can be used to protect the Apaches from enemy aircraft.

"DISCO LIGHT" JAMMER

The jammer sends out signals that confuse heat-seeking missiles.

LONGBOW RADAR

The Longbow radar is used to pick up enemy radar signals and find out where they are.

RADAR JAMMER

This jammer is used to send false information to enemy radar.

EXHAUST

The hot exhaust gases are mixed with cooler air before they leave the aircraft.

WIRE CUTTERS

The Apache has six wire cutters on the front to cut any electric wires that it may hit.

MISSILES

The Apache's most important weapon is the Hellfire missile. The Hellfire is used against tanks and missile sites.

The Hellfire missiles can be fired slightly upward over small hills or other obstacles. Once the Longbow radar has found the target, the Apache can stay hidden while it fires the Hellfire missiles.

The Apache's missiles make it possible to attack an enemy that is far away. Guns and rockets can only be used when the enemy is close.

This Apache has a Hellfire mounted next to a rocket launcher. The Apache carries up to 16 Hellfires.

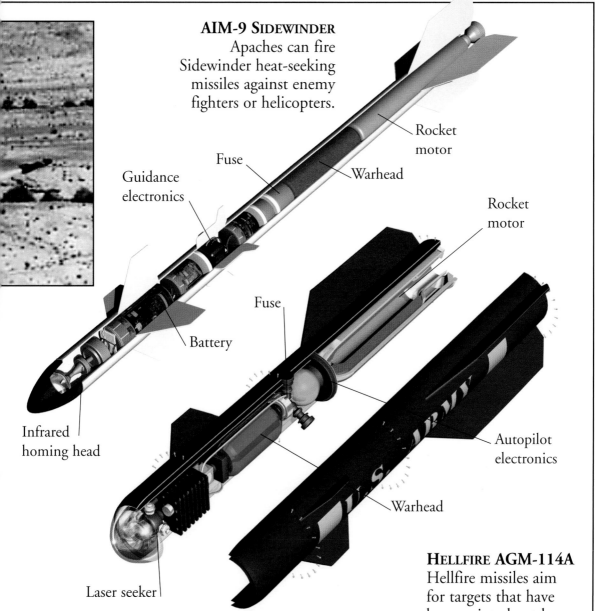

AIM-9 SIDEWINDER
Apaches can fire Sidewinder heat-seeking missiles against enemy fighters or helicopters.

Rocket motor

Fuse

Warhead

Guidance electronics

Rocket motor

Battery

Fuse

Infrared homing head

Autopilot electronics

Warhead

Laser seeker

HELLFIRE AGM-114A
Hellfire missiles aim for targets that have been pointed out by laser. The name is short for HELicopter-Launched FIRE-and-forget missile. "Forget" means that once fired, the Hellfire does not need crew control to find its target.

When the missiles are fired, they automatically find their targets. The Apache moves on immediately to avoid enemy fire aimed at the point from which the missiles were fired.

GUNS AND ROCKETS

At closer ranges, the Apache attacks targets on the ground with unguided rockets or its 30 mm gun.

The rockets are fired from launchers that each contain 19 rockets. The rockets are smaller and simpler weapons than the Hellfire missiles.

M230
CHAIN GUN

The 30 mm gun is set under the nose and steered by the gunner.

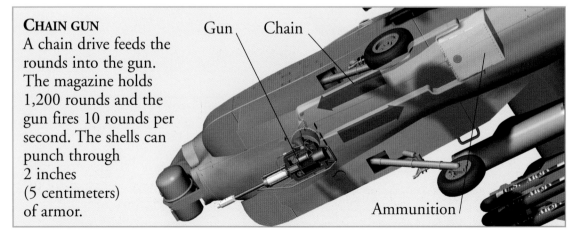

CHAIN GUN
A chain drive feeds the rounds into the gun. The magazine holds 1,200 rounds and the gun fires 10 rounds per second. The shells can punch through 2 inches (5 centimeters) of armor.

Gun   Chain

Ammunition

ROCKETS

Different rockets are used for different tasks. Multi-purpose rockets shower enemy vehicles with deadly pieces. Shaped charges are used to punch through the armor on an enemy vehicle. The illumination rocket lights up the night over an area of nearly one-half mile (.8 kilometer) for almost 2 minutes.

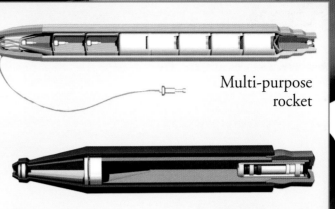

Multi-purpose rocket

Shaped charge

The 30 mm gun is a powerful weapon. Each round takes just 2 seconds to travel 3,281 feet (1,000 meters).

If the helicopter crashes, the gun is designed to fold up into an empty space between the pilot and gunner so that it does not go off inside and harm them.

ROCKET LAUNCHER

The rocket launchers are set on the stub wings, like the Hellfire missile. Once the rockets have been launched, small fins spring out to help the rockets in flight.

THE MISSION

As we have seen, Apaches are well suited as combat helicopters.

A typical mission, shown here, shows how Apaches hide behind hills and large rocks while they find their target. Apaches surprise their enemy and get away quickly to avoid being shot down.

1. Two Longbow Apaches are sent out on a mission to find enemy tanks thought to be in the area.

5. The Apaches disappear as fast as possible behind the hill to avoid enemy fire. They return to base.

2. A Marine Harrier that is returning from a mission spots the tanks. The Harrier pilot immediately reports what he has seen.

3. The Apaches approach the tanks. They know where the enemy is and fly low behind the hill to avoid being seen.

2

3

4

4. The Apaches suddenly strike. They attack the enemy tanks with Hellfire missiles.

THE FUTURE

The Apache will continue to be an important weapon for many years. It can move easily and quickly, making it hard to shoot down. The Apache can also attack many targets.

The radio and computers on the Apache will probably be updated. Updates will help the crew to keep better contact with fighters in the air and with tanks and troops on the ground.

There are also plans for unmanned aircraft that would fly ahead of the Apaches. These aircraft could help Apaches find enemy tanks and air defenses.

Knowing the exact location of both the enemy and your own troops is very important on the battlefield.

Better contact with friendly tanks on the ground is one way of improving the Apache.

The X-45A is an
unmanned aircraft.

GLOSSARY

avionics (ay-vee-ON-iks)—the electronics in an aircraft

chaff (CHAF)—thin strips of metal that are released into the air to confuse a radar-controlled missile

cockpit (KOK-pit)—the cabin surrounded by windows where the pilot sits; the Apache has a two-person cockpit.

Hellfire missile (HEL-fire MISS-uhl)—a missile that, once launched, does not need crew control to find its target; it is the Apache's most important weapon.

horsepower (HORSS-pou-ur)—the measurement of an engine's power, abbreviated as hp

Longbow radar (LONG-boh RAY-dar)—equipment that uses radio waves to pick up and locate enemy radar signals

rotor (ROH-tur)—blades like rotating wings that lift the helicopter and control its direction

Sidewinder missile (SIDE-winde-er MISS-uhl)—a missile that finds its target by the heat the target gives out

torque (TORK)—the force that makes a helicopter turn in the opposite direction to the main rotor

READ MORE

Dartford, Mark. *Helicopters.* Military Hardware in Action. Minneapolis: Lerner, 2003.

Sweetman, Bill. *Attack Helicopters: The AH-64 Apaches.* War Planes. Mankato, Minn.: Capstone Press, 2001.

Tetrick, Byron. *Choosing a Career as a Pilot.* World of Work. New York: Rosen, 2002.

INTERNET SITES

FactHound offers a safe, fun way to find Internet sites related to this book. All of the sites on FactHound have been researched by our staff.

Here's how:
1. Visit *www.facthound.com*
2. Type in this special code **0736852506** for age-appropriate sites. Or enter a search word related to this book for a more general search.
3. Click on the **Fetch It** button.

FactHound will fetch the best sites for you!

INDEX